Conversations
with
Nature

YOU'RE INVITED TO JOIN THE *C*ONVERSATION.

To Suzanne Gunning, my school teacher,
who championed and nurtured my
writing from childhood.

CONTENTS

The Tree	1
A Lonely Little Girl	2
The Hermit and The Heron	4
Eye to Luminous Eye	6
Urban Refugee	7
I'll Be Dammed	10
When Joy Takes Wing	11
The Heart of the Honey	14
Into The Nether	15
Writhes and Wriggles	18
Silent Flight	20

INTRODUCTION

In a world driven by constant noise, consumption, and the relentless pursuit of more, *Conversations with Nature* is an invitation to pause.

Through poetic reflections, this collection offers a soft rebellion against the fast-paced, profit-driven systems that disconnect us from ourselves and the world around us.

Each creature and landscape in these pages invites you into a deep conversation; an intimate dialogue that reminds you that you belong to something far greater than any man-made structure or system. You are woven into the fabric of this Earth.

This book has found you for a reason. In nature, nothing is accidental. And you, are indeed, part of nature.

Let these words be a call to slow down, to listen, and to rediscover the freedom in simply being.

You're never alone; you are, and always have been, an integral part of this living, breathing tapestry.

So, come as you are, join the conversation and let these pages wrap around you like an old friend. We're so glad you're here!

THE TREE

As above, so below,
And everywhere I go.
The air I breathe, the leaves I see—
What's without is also within me.

The tree has layers,
And so do I. Roots and lines,
Intricate patterns I've seen before—
Fingerprints upon the door.
Rings and crypts, veins and vines,
Individuals expressed
Through universal designs.

I am you, you are me;
In vast, radiant woods, I am the tree.

A LONELY LITTLE GIRL

To dance a million dances,
to sing a thousand songs,
to laugh and cry in places
in which I don't belong.

I force polite smiles to creatures
that warrant my distaste,
but I still show up,
I do the work
and put on my best face.

But behind the row of houses
and buildings that touch the sky,
I often sit at river edges
and begin to ponder why:

Why my best friends have branches
and my enemies have hands,
Why my soulmate speaks in whispers
and grows upon the land.

Why currents swirl like little dancers
whirling down the stream,
Why the last time my feet touched water
was merely in a dream,

Why mallard ducks sit distanced,
perched upon the rocks
And, of course, it's human nature
that wedges as it knocks.

The trees, they do not discriminate,
even when out of line.
They're the only friendship that I have found
that stands the test of time.

The leaves do not hold grudges
as they allow themselves to grow;
they do their duty, they say "goodbye,"
and once again, "hello."

When asked if I am lonely
as I spend my time alone,
I am comforted every day
by the things that I've never known.

I have found my peace inside myself
and that in which I know,
and more so in the things I don't,
aware that they're soon to show.

I find my friends in the soil
that caress my feet below,
not in the pubs with strangers
whose stories are of woe.

And if that makes me lonely
and distanced from this world,
I remember I was closer to the earth
when I was once a lonely little girl.

THE HERMIT & THE HERON

I take my place on the rocks next to the hunch of sleek silvery plumes. Neither of us flinch. Moments pass and we exchange a few glances. Nothing interrupts us from our nothingness.

The still river edges to the brink of tormenting quiet. Maybe even... peaceful. Just along the small, rocky coast, ducks undocked, with their little paddles charging full steam ahead. To the high seas they go — and they just had to shout about it. My slender friend remains undisturbed. Unshaken by the tiny ripples of a lively tide. Unswayed to join the commotion. Temptation has no hold on its coiling neck. I observe that in nothing, it says everything. In its not-doing, it was doing so much.

Why wouldn't it join them? Why would it choose to wade these shallow waters in solitude? Loneliness. Isolation. Completely alienated from the skips of jovial magpies and boisterous bobbings of paddling ducks. It remains like a sharp pin perched between the coolness of a River Clyde evening. Diligent and discerning. Expending no energy on the futile distractions of its surroundings. And when it speared its prey in a sudden jolt, quicker than my eye could observe, it answered.

"What good would it do a duck, a stout, rounded forager, to waddle its webs in swampy marshland? It can't do my job, and I won't do its. I wish them well on the high seas, but a duck would flounder in my role. Not because it lacks purpose, but because its purpose is different."

I think of the many people I'd wandered away from to sit upon the rocks with my feathered reflection. I think of the many ducks I'd tried to be, and hardly survived — grazing only on the surface when I was made for the depths.

There, on the edge of this vast river, we were both silent seekers fulfilling our roles. Solitude takes courage, and like the heron, I no longer concerned myself with the fast bobbings of ducks. My heart in steady rhythm with the low beat of its soft blankets of icy blues, I had come to embrace the shelter of my cave. No longer scary, but necessary. Maybe even...peaceful. I understood.

Staying true to my nature was staying true to *my* nature.

EYE TO LUMINOUS EYE

For the first time in my life, I am level with something bigger than myself. Something bigger than all I've ever known – the moon.

It sits as a silvery disk on the horizon, spotlighting the strokes of cloud beneath, and for a moment, I envisioned a polished and gleaming stage upon which, I was so eager to perform. *But, it's night time*, I remind myself.

For once, this was not a foreign force residing overhead, keeping a very silent watch on my most vulnerable hours. No, this felt like someone I could've known.

I love the moon, I say to myself as I pass it on the plane.

It meets me with delicate frosty whispers, and unlike the sun, doesn't shout my name. It alludes *to much*, without giving *that much* away. It knows more than it's letting on. I sense *as much*.

And, to the moon, I asked: *What will tomorrow bring? What have you seen? And, who has seen you? How many people must've met with you! And, up here, thousands of feet in the air, you meet with me.*

I look around to make sure that it is, indeed, me it is meeting with. Heads are buried and yielding to the invisible pressure of their fatigue. Shoulders have collapsed into a vibrant sea of laundry. It is, like I had wished, just me and the moon. Eye to luminous eye.

I have met you in many, many lives, I think.

URBAN REFUGEE

Took myself down to the smoky bar on the corner,
And to the old boys and bankers, I'm a stick-out foreigner.
But I know it won't be long until I belong there,
Just need to find a button-up and fedora to hide my orange hair.

Through the hum of crowds and past the bustle,
Sat the poker men and their talks of hustle,
How only strong men are made out of muscle,
And a heart's not worth the torture of the tussle.

Tonight is the first time I'm in disguise,
Blending and mending before empty eyes,
My obsidian nose reflecting all their lies,
My pointed ears drowning in my babies' cries.

That's when I seen the sulking man approach me,
Place a cigar between my lips and let him stone me,
But instead he asked if he could know me,
And some kindly company, I guess, he could loan me.

My husky voice began...

"I used to feast myself fancy in the big country,
And everywhere I went, I spent my money,
But since bosses came knocking for their company,
I've had to make my weary way into this city.

All my neighbours used to cry about me leaving,
'I wonder what they'll do if they catch you thieving,'
But for my losses, I've never spent much time grieving,
For a better future, you must know, I still believe in."

Hand on chest, he replied...

"I come in peace, my dear friend, I'm not a foe,
I don't wield weapons on the land where your young grow,
And though my heart is heavy, I'll take your blow,
But indeed, it's the man above me, not below."

There I sat beside a lonesome soul about my age,
Whose manager's making him work for minimum wage.
"What's it like to be crammed in the corporate cage?"
But I knew the sorry answer he could not face.

Cooly, I said...

"I've come to see, you're a puppet on a string.
And what an almighty pain to your soul that must bring,
But to the concrete jungle, you all cling,
And I patiently await the pendulum swing."

In glazed eyes, he revealed his feeble fears...

"Truth be told, I've not seen the night sky in many years.
I have waited all this time for it to clear,
But clarity is not bestowed through casks of beer.

In the city, we wait a lifetime for night to come,
But we've gone all cerebral drinking rum,
Waiting to feast on the big bosses' crumbs,
And evade the beating of nature's drums."

Finally, I responded...

"Though I hear you, good man, you're not alone.
But the industry you submit to has taken my home.
Through golden fields, I can no longer roam,
And my flaky fur is fading to its bone."

I lifted my hat to reveal what was kept,
And from the leather seat, the sulking man leapt.
His forehead dowsed in guilty sweat,
The sulking man knew the sins he'd swept.

"I fear you must've met me long before,
Tip-toeing in your garden, past your door,
Swarming dusty bins while you snore,
I'm the foreign fox on the street that you ignore."

I'LL BE DAMMED

"I'll be dammed," said the beaver through gritted teeth.

It gnawed and stacked, piece by careful piece.
The river rose high, unforgivingly consuming
every weak design in its wake.

Twigs and branches speared through the current,
and the dry mud beneath me
moulded to marshland.

I watched on, captivated by nature's finest engineer.
Its rusty saws sunk into surrounding bark.
A fortress of purpose,
built in the midst of forever shifting sands.

How does it do it? I asked.

"Foundations, my friend," it replied.

Discarding my sinking stilts from below,
I laid my lost body to rest upon the sturdy boulder
beside me.

Foundations, indeed, I replied.

WHEN JOY TAKES WING

Every day, gone ten o'clock,
I meet the magpie on my walk.
We strut for miles, side by side,
Yet one thought lingers in my mind:

I'm slow with strides and full of grace,
Encumbered by pride, so stiff in pace.
I envy my friend and his little hops,
That carry him lightly on woodland stops.

Monday comes, and he says to me,
"It's warm today—let's play by the sea."
I scoff at his offer, straighten my coat,
Assured that my pride won't keep me afloat.

Tuesday arrives, and he tries again:
"Let's hop or jump, my solemn friend."
I scoff once more and point at my shoes,
"Oh, I could never," say my Tuesday blues.

Wednesday greets me with a sullen hello,
"Come on, let's see how far you'll go."
I scoff at the rain and shake my head,
Certain the distance would bring me dread.

Thursday knocks and pulls me from bed:
"Today, let's taste the apples instead."
I scoff and point down the wooded straight,
Determined our walk could not be late.

Friday dawns, with the sun in play,
"Let's stop and smell the roses today!"
I pinch my nose, ensuring it's closed,
And march ahead, as my pride imposed.

Saturday swells with bustling groups,
"Let's sift through the gifts that the west wind loops!"
I glance at my watch and quickly decline—
Evading joy, right on time.

Sunday appears, a quiet, clear day;
I scheme of reasons to keep joy at bay.
But no magpie greets me, no song in the air,
And the silence lingers, heavy and bare.

I search through the bushes, paddle the sea,
Wishing my friend were here with me.
I'd leap to the sky and fling arms wide,
To welcome the joy I've long denied.

I'd taste every fruit the kind trees have grown,
Fly with the birds where their songs have flown,
Smell every rose and cherish the breeze,
And thank my friend for teaching me these.

In the distance, I see his flight—
A streak of feathers, black and white.
He sees my arms and circles down,
To meet his friend who's dropped their frown.

Now I know, there's no perfect time
To taste life's nectar or sip its wine.
Tear down the walls, brick by brick,
And let joy find you, for sweetness will stick.

We don't have long on this green earth,
So claim the joy that's been yours since birth.
It's not just fleeting or here for a day—
Joy is yours, and it's here to stay.

THE HEART OF THE HONEY

My cupboard has never housed expired honey—a sustainable indulgence. But its constant presence bore a niggling question: *Who was at the heart of it?*

As the bleaker months drew closer and little critters sought shelter, I began to miss the gentle hum of my garden's most hardworking friends: the bees. I looked around at the barren world—leafless trees, fading colours—and panic set in.

Summer was a delightful feast, a tank full of fuel. I basked in its fruits, over and over, until I unknowingly brought myself an early winter. Reserves now running empty.

The heart of the honey is not a fleeting buzz, but a long, gentle hum. Enduring. Its gold sustains a hive through the scarcest months.

As the silver settles outside, I long for golden honey in these empty chambers—a heart sticky with sustained sweetness. A reminder of what it means to endure.

To hold, in the quiet of winter, a sweetness that doesn't fade.

INTO THE NETHER

Bottomless pit, I despair your call,
Into the Nether, must I fall?

The Great Unknown, the greatest risk,
Slowly, slowly, the Great Abyss.

I scathe and scratch, to no avail,
Flipping, flapping, a flounder's tail.

The ocean opens, it asks for me,
Deeper, deeper, the darkest sea.

No light, no sight, no smell, no sound,
Submerged and swallowed by the underground.

When from the cold, I heard its siren,
Further, further, the fading horizon.

Who is this? What is your song?
In this ocean, I don't belong.

So, give me comfort, it's what I seek,
Softly, softly, it began to speak:

"I'm thick with blubber and icy blue,
I've come to share this journey with you.

It's long and treacherous, so lighten your load,
Beneath my fin, your shelter's bestowed."

Fumbling and falling, I reached for the dark,
Trusting the whale, and fearing a shark.

Immersing myself in its titan creation,
Closer, closer, the great migration.

"I sense you poor soul, you resist the pit,
But real danger dwells where two worlds doth split.

Above the ocean, below the sky,
On the Great Green Earth, your troubles will lie...

...They'll linger there, like relics long kept,
Taunting and haunting, where old demons slept.

So trust this journey, though shadows fall,
In darkness, the sound of your spirit will call.

To emerge from the sea, in all your glory,
And with the world, you'll share this story,

Of what was found in the rugged depths,
Are all the things the ego has swept."

Time had passed, and all endured,
Strength was gained and pain was cured.

Quick with action, slow in rest,
Fonder, fonder, of these icy depths.

Through raging storms, and foreceful tide,
the giant swam close at side.

When from above, formed glimmers of light,
Finally, finally, I gained my sight.

WRITHES & WRIGGLES

Autumn comes with writhes and wriggles,
And aches I can't explain.
And the more I fumble for the answers,
The longer I'm in pain.

For I know the recipe to my cure
Is stored in letting go,
But the more I tend to think about it,
The less I seem to know.

Before me in the mirror,
Lays a creature scaled in green,
And many portraits of itself
Its ochre eyes have seen.

And as its skin is shedding,
Its process it did loathe,
And it often wondered to itself:
"Is this the price of growth?"

The tales of toxic venom
Which trickle from its fangs,
Paint a vivid picture
On the wall in which it hangs.

It tells me it won't visit there,
The gallery of pain.
Not until its final scale,
That liberates its shame.

I want to ask it questions,
And probe its critter mind:
"What's it like to go in circles,
Always chasing what's behind?"

"Do you know your tail is part of you,
Hate it as you may?
And its taunting little shadow
Is not what's in your way..."

Use your ochre eyes, my friend,
Resist the wince and hiss,
And from this process you may find
That shedding *is* the bliss.

Those words were music to the ears,
Of a snake who did resist.
But it turned to me with a solemn smile:
"So, this is what it's like to exist...

Here! In this very moment,
When I'm not chasing my teasing tail,
Nor focused on the new skin growing,
Afraid that it may frail...

So long as I keep shedding,
And embrace this ache and pain,
I'll surrender to the writhes and wriggles
That no one need explain."

SILENT FLIGHT

A moonlit walk through midnight blue,
My mind is scattered, my heart's askew.
But sitting there, beyond the trees,
There, perched, an owl with plumage of leaves.

Divulge your secrets of the great unknown,
Through many storms those feathers have flown,
While many birds are nestled on fences,
You, Great Owl, have heightened your senses.

"Ah, in scattered motion, runs busy prey,
While I take shelter on a busy day.
I'm quiet in movement, silent in flight,
I come to life on a silent night.

Yes, the early bird catches the worm,
Through every toss and violent turn,
But unlike others, I forsake the light,
I revere in the dark and its gift of foresight."

I see in silence, what once was concealed,
The answers I sought are now revealed.
My neck arched back, my hands to the night,
I thanked the owl on its silent flight.

ABOUT THE AUTHOR

Ailsa Gillies was born on the Isle of Bute, a small island on the west coast of Scotland. Her love for words began early, and at just 9 years old, she won a local poetry competition by reciting Robert Burns' *To a Mouse*.

At 17, Ailsa left her island home to pursue studies in Journalism, Film, and Media, earning her Master's degree by the age of 22. She was first published at 19, contributing to various local and national publications, including BBC Scotland's *The Social*.

Now based in Erskine, Ailsa has traded the corporate grind for quieter life immersed in nature, where she runs her own website *Ailsa Gillies Editorial*. Her writing is deeply inspired by the landscapes of her homeland, her connection to the natural world and her ongoing quest for meaning and joy in simplicity as a soft rebellion against a world that demands more, more, more.

Printed in Great Britain
by Amazon